WORK

For

THE SOURCE

The Secrets Of The Universe, The Science
Of The Brain.

A Practical Guide To Tara Swart's Book.

Amazing Publisher

This Book Belongs To:

Disclaimer

This workbook is an unofficial companion to the original book. It's not endorsed, sponsored, or associated with the original author or publisher of the original book. All views and opinions expressed in this workbook are those of the author and do not necessarily reflect the views and the opinions of the author or publisher of the original book.

HOW TO USE THIS WORKBOOK

Congratulations on commencing on your adventure with "The Source" by Tara Swart! This workbook is meant to supplement your reading experience and help you enhance your grasp of the important topics given in the book. Here's how you can properly utilize this workbook:

1. Key Lessons: Take the time to read and think on the major lessons presented for each chapter. These lessons give significant insights and serve as the framework for your research of the book's subjects.

2. Self-Reflection Questions: Engage with the self-reflection questions to tailor your learning experience. These questions are meant to stimulate reflection and help you apply the book's ideas to your own life.

3. Food For Thought: Consider the food for thought suggestions as encouragement to broaden your thinking and examine the book's topics from multiple viewpoints.

Use these suggestions to generate fresh thoughts and increase your grasp of the content.

4. Application: As you go through the workbook, consider how you may apply the lessons and insights to your everyday life. Think about practical measures you may take to incorporate the book's ideas into your routines and habits.

5. Journaling: Consider maintaining a diary to chronicle your ideas, comments, and discoveries as you proceed through the workbook. Writing may be a great instrument for self-discovery and personal progress.

Remember, the workbook is designed to be a tool to complement and enrich your reading experience with "The Source." Embrace the process, be open to new discoveries, and enjoy the path of discovery and self-exploration!

Table of
Content

Table of
Content

INTRODUCTION

"The Source" by Tara Swart is a riveting investigation of the deep relationship between the human brain, the cosmos, and the keys to unleashing our full potential. Through a combination of neuroscience, psychology, and spiritual knowledge, Swart delivers a fascinating story that walks readers on a transforming journey towards discovering and unleashing the power inside themselves.

The book is structured into various parts, each presenting unique insights and practical solutions for personal development and self-discovery. Let's go into a synopsis of the important ideas and chapters discussed:

1. The Law Of Attraction: Swart exposes readers to the notion of the Law of Attraction, highlighting the significance of our thoughts and beliefs in influencing our world. By matching our intentions with the energy of the cosmos, we may materialize our wants and attain our objectives.

2. Visualize It: In this chapter, Swart investigates the role of vision in activating the subconscious mind and realizing our dreams. By developing vivid mental representations of our desired goals, we may train our brains for success and attract wonderful events into our lives.

3. Your Amazing Brain: Genesis Of The Source: Swart digs into the intriguing area of neurology, showing how our brains are built for success and progress. By knowing the science underlying our brain's powers, we may tap into its full potential and release the power of "The Source" inside us.

4. Your Malleable Mind: How To Rewire Your Neural Pathways: This chapter covers the notion of neuroplasticity, showing the brain's incredible capacity to adapt and evolve throughout our lifetimes.

5. Brain Agility: How To Nimbly Switch Between Different Types Of Thinking: Swart emphasizes the necessity of cognitive agility in negotiating the difficulties of contemporary life. By improving the capacity to move between multiple modes of thinking, we may boost our creativity, problem-solving abilities, and flexibility.

6. Emotions: Master Your Feelings: In this chapter, Swart analyzes the science of emotions and their influence on our mental and physical well-being. By managing our emotions and growing emotional intelligence, we may lead more satisfying and balanced lives.

7. Physically: Know Yourself: Swart highlights the role of physical health and well-being in boosting brain performance. By adopting healthy lifestyle habits, such as correct eating, exercise, and sleep, we can promote our brain's health and unleash its full potential.

8. Intuition: Trust Your Gut: Swart investigates the value of intuition as a vital tool for decision-making and handling life's difficulties. By following our inner knowledge and intuition, we may make decisions that connect with our real selves and lead to greater satisfaction.

9. Motivation: Stay Resilient To Achieve Your Goals: In this chapter, Swart addresses the science of motivation and resilience, suggesting suggestions for remaining focused and motivated in the pursuit of our objectives. By understanding the neurobiology of motivation, we may overcome hurdles and attain success.

Each chapter of "The Source" contains useful insights, practical activities, and thought-provoking reflections meant to inspire readers to unleash their full potential and live a life aligned with their greatest wishes. By combining the ideas and practices contained in the book, readers may go on a journey of self-discovery, personal development, and change.

The Law Of Attraction

Key Lessons:

1. Your Thoughts Shape Your Reality: Understanding that your ideas contain a magnetic nature, attracting similar energy, is crucial. Every thought gives forth a distinct vibration that helps to forming your reality.

2. The Power of Positive Intentions: Delve into the transforming potential of optimistic intentions. The Law of Attraction reacts to the energy you create; so, developing happy ideas may manifest favorable consequences in your life.

3. Aligning Your Subconscious Mind: Uncover the value of harmonizing your conscious and subconscious brains. The Law of Attraction acts on both levels, and aligning them improves your potential to materialize your wishes.

4. Emotional Resonance: Explore the function of emotions in the manifestation process. Emotional resonance amplifies the vibrational frequency of your ideas, affecting the attraction of comparable events.

5. Practical Application in Daily Life: Implementing the Law of Attraction in your everyday practice is vital. Discover practical activities and approaches that Tara Swart advises for incorporating these ideas into your life successfully.

Self-Refelction Questions:

1 .How can you become more conscious of your prevailing ideas and their influence on your experiences?

_____

_____

_____

_____

_____

_____

2. What beliefs or thought patterns can be impeding the manifestation of your objectives, and how can you replace them with empowered ones?

_____

_____

_____

_____

_____

_____

3. What measures can you take to create a more positive mentality and connect your beliefs with the results you desire?

_____

_____

_____

_____

_____

_____

4. How can you develop harmony between your conscious and subconscious thoughts to boost the efficiency of the Law of Attraction in your life?

_____

_____

_____

_____

_____

_____

_____

5. Reflect on the feelings you regularly encounter. How do you guarantee that your emotions correspond with the good results you intend to attract?

FOOD FOR THOUGHT

1. Consider how your ideas not only touch your immediate reality but also send out energy waves that may alter the world around you.

2. Ponder on the concept that constant use of the Law of Attraction is vital. How can you build a daily habit that fosters positive thinking?

3. Reflect on obstacles as chances to develop your views and aspirations. How do you retain a good outlook in the midst of adversity?

4. Contemplate the function of visualizing in manifesting aspirations. How can you include vivid mental images into your everyday routine to quicken the manifestation process?

5. Consider the powerful influence of appreciation on the Law of Attraction. How can expressing appreciation become a cornerstone of your everyday mindset?

KEYNOTES

Visualize It

Key Lessons:

1. Your capacity to imagine with clarity directly determines the efficiency of manifestation. Learn to improve and concentrate your imagination for clearer and more effective images.

2. Understand the significant influence of emotions on your visions. The more emotionally invested you are in the process, the more strong the manifestation becomes.

3. Visualization acts as a technique to develop a thorough mental blueprint of your intended objectives. Learn how to build a vivid and powerful picture in your mind to direct the manifestation process.

4. Consistent visualization is crucial to integrating your desires into your subconscious mind. Explore tactics and habits that make visualization a regular and productive part of your everyday life.

5. Visualization is most potent when accompanied with motivated action. Learn how to easily incorporate your imagined results into your everyday actions to speed their manifestation.

Self-Refelction Questions:

1. How can you boost the accuracy of your visualizations to provide a more accurate portrayal of your targeted outcomes?

_____

_____

_____

_____

_____

2. How can you strengthen the emotional involvement in your visions to magnify their influence on your subconscious mind?

_____

_____

_____

_____

_____

_____

_____

3. What measures can you take to develop a more vivid and comprehensive mental blueprint for your objectives via visualization?

_____

_____

_____

_____

_____

4. How can you include visualization into your everyday practice to create a continuous and powerful manifestation process?

_____

_____

_____

_____

_____

5. Reflect on how you might match your everyday activities with the pictured outcomes, making them an intrinsic part of your path towards your objectives.

_____

_____

_____

_____

_____

_____

_____

_____

_____

_____

_____

_____

_____

FOOD FOR THOUGHT

1. Consider how tiny alterations in your visualization method may lead to substantial shifts in your view of and approach to your objectives.

2. Ponder on the thought that the good energy created by visualization transcends beyond your own experiences, impacting the world around you.

3. Explore how visualization may serve not just as a manifestation tool but also as a great approach for controlling stress and building a happy mentality.

4. Reflect on the notion of enjoying tiny accomplishments along your path, understanding how persistent visualizing adds to these incremental achievements.

5. Consider how envisioning the full process, including the hurdles and progress, might strengthen your resilience and dedication to accomplishing your objectives.

KEYNOTES

Your Amazing Brain: Genesis Of The Source

Key Lessons:

1. Your brain's potential for neuroplasticity allows for ongoing development and adaptation. Understand how this function offers unlimited opportunities for personal and spiritual growth.

2. Recognize that your brain is not just a processing unit; it is a source of energy that interacts with the universal consciousness. Explore how this link shapes your experiences.

3. Learn about the synergistic interaction between your mind and body. The balance between these aspects is vital for unlocking the full power of your brain and uniting with the global source.

4. Explore the connection between neuroscience and spirituality. Tara Swart elucidates how knowing the brain's mechanics may strengthen your spiritual connection and vice versa.

5. Your brain is the core of your general well-being. Delve into the holistic approach to health, considering the importance of mental, emotional, and spiritual components on your brain's optimum performance.

Self-Refelction Questions:

1. How can you harness your brain's neuroplasticity to support continual growth and progress in all facets of your life?

_____

_____

_____

_____

_____

_____

2. What modifications can you make in your daily routine to maximize the energy flow from your brain and align it with the universal source?

_____

_____

_____

_____

_____

_____

3. Reflect on how your mind and body presently interact. What techniques can you use to strengthen their harmony for better well-being?

_____

_____

_____

_____

_____

4. How can you connect the ideas of neuroscience and spirituality to expand your knowledge of both domains and raise your spiritual experience?

_____

_____

_____

_____

_____

_____

5. What holistic activities can you undertake to nurture not just your mental and emotional health but also to promote the proper functioning of your brain and its connection to the universal source?

_____

_____

_____

_____

_____

_____

_____

_____

_____

_____

_____

_____

FOOD FOR THOUGHT

1. Contemplate the thought that your brain has endless potential for development and evolution. How does this revelation encourage a transformation in your outlook on personal development?

2. Ponder on the thought that your brain actively helps to forming your experience. How can you leverage this understanding to produce great results in your life?

3. Consider the enormous interdependence between your intellect and spiritual experiences. How does recognizing this link effect your approach to personal growth?

4. Reflect on the techniques that replenish and increase the energy pouring from your brain. How can you prioritize these habits in your everyday life?

5. Explore the merits of taking a holistic approach to well-being. How can you weave together mental, emotional, and spiritual aspects to create a tapestry of holistic wellness in your life?

KEYNOTES

Your Malleable Mind: How To Rewire Your Neural Pathways

Key Lessons:

1. Embrace the notion that your brain contains the unique power of neuronal plasticity. Recognize this as your superpower for molding ideas, actions, and eventually, your life.

2. Delve into the potential of repetition in rewiring brain networks. Learn how consistent thoughts and behaviors may build enduring changes in your brain's structure and functioning.

3. Understand the value of conscious attention in the rewiring process. Your mind is a sculptor, and by focusing concentrated attention, you may change brain connections to coincide with your objectives.

4. Explore how emotions act as effective anchors in rewiring. Understand their role in memory formation and how attaching positive emotions to new pathways can expedite the transformation.

5. Dive into the relationship between neuroplasticity and habit development. Uncover how actively rearranging your brain pathways may enable the establishment of beneficial and powerful behaviors.

Self-Refelction Questions:

1. How can you actively use the potential of neuronal plasticity in transforming your beliefs, habits, and life outcomes?

_____

_____

_____

_____

_____

_____

2. What recurrent ideas or activities now impact your brain pathways, and how can you actively adjust them for good change?

_____

_____

_____

_____

_____

_____

3. In what areas of your life might purposeful attention lead to big transformations? How do you nurture this attention to rebuild your brain circuits effectively?

_____

_____

_____

_____

_____

4. Reflect on the emotions related to your present ambitions. How can you improve pleasant emotions to function as anchors in remodeling brain pathways for success?

_____

_____

_____

_____

_____

5. Which habits do you desire to acquire, and how can you intentionally utilize neuroplasticity to hasten their production and integration into your everyday life?

_____

_____

_____

_____

_____

_____

_____

_____

_____

_____

_____

_____

_____

FOOD FOR THOUGHT

1. Consider the dynamic nature of your brain and its continual flexibility. How does this knowledge generate a feeling of empowerment and opportunity for good change?

2. Ponder on the thought that constancy is the brushstroke in the masterpiece of brain remodeling. How can you inject persistent effort into altering your brain pathways?

3. Explore the influence of incorporating good emotions into your objectives. How can you purposefully develop and magnify happy emotions to expedite your brain rewiring journey?

4. Reflect on the deliberate development of focused attention. How might a deliberate approach to your thoughts and behaviors increase the success of your brain rewiring endeavors?

5. Consider the lifetime process of neuronal rewiring for growth. How can you accept this path as a constant process of self-improvement and evolution?

KEYNOTES

_____

_____

_____

_____

_____

_____

_____

_____

_____

_____

_____

_____

_____

_____

_____

_____

Brain Agility: How To Nimbly Switch Between Different Types Of Thinking

Key Lessons:

1. Discover the power of adjusting your thinking approach to meet the nature of situations. Learn how a quick transition between analytical, creative, and strategic thinking may enhance problem-solving.

2. Understand the function of neurotransmitters in creating your thinking processes. Explore how neurotransmitter balance influences your ability to easily shift between various modes of thought.

3. Cultivate conscious awareness of your thinking habits. Recognize when you are stuck into a certain thought pattern and build techniques to intentionally transition to a more suited approach.

4. Leverage neuroplasticity to boost your brain's adaptability. Appreciate how intentionally participating in varied thought activities may change brain connections and increase cognitive flexibility.

5. Explore how your surroundings effects your thoughts. Recognize the value of establishing favorable environments that encourage the style of thinking necessary for various activities or obstacles.

Self-Refelction Questions:

1. How can you become more competent at matching your thinking style with the unique issues you meet, encouraging more effective problem-solving?

_____

_____

_____

_____

_____

2. In what ways can you encourage a healthy mix of neurotransmitters in your brain to assist smooth transitions between various forms of thinking?

_____

_____

_____

_____

_____

_____

3. How can you strengthen your attentive awareness of your cognitive patterns, assuring a more deliberate and purposeful approach to your thought processes?

_____

_____

_____

_____

_____

4. What various cognitive tasks can you intentionally participate in to exploit neuroplasticity and boost your brain's general versatility?

_____

_____

_____

_____

_____

5. Reflect on your existing settings. How can you arrange and improve your environment to encourage the sort of thinking necessary for optimum cognitive agility?

_____

_____

_____

_____

_____

_____

_____

_____

_____

_____

_____

_____

_____

FOOD FOR THOUGHT

1. Consider your thinking patterns as instruments in a symphony. How do you arrange these approaches together to generate a balanced and productive cognitive performance?

2. Ponder on the concept of neurotransmitters as conductors arranging your brain's symphony. How can you achieve a balanced and well-coordinated cognitive function via lifestyle choices?

3. Reflect on neuroplasticity as a dance between your ideas and your brain's structure. How does this dance affect your capacity to adapt and learn in varied situations?

4. Explore the notion of intentionally switching between cognitive modes. How can you become more purposeful in managing these changes to enhance your cognitive agility?

5. Consider your surroundings as a thinking partner. How can you create settings that inspire and encourage the unique thinking types essential for your everyday work and challenges?

KEYNOTES

Emotions: Master Your Feelings

Key Lessons:

1. Recognize that emotional intelligence is the key to managing your emotions. Develop a deep awareness of your emotions to manage life's obstacles with perseverance and grace.

2. Understand the symbiotic interaction between ideas and emotions. Acknowledge how your ideas impact your emotional reactions and discover techniques to moderate and redirect them.

3. Explore the fundamental mind-body link in emotional mastery. Cultivate activities that build harmony between your mental and physical states, helping you to manage your emotions successfully.

4. Develop skills for handling unpleasant emotions productively. Embrace obstacles as chances to learn and develop, harnessing adversity to improve your emotional resilience.

5. Acknowledge the transforming power of expressing your feelings. Discover healthy channels for emotional release, encouraging a balanced and true experience of your emotions.

Self-Refelction Questions:

1. How can you expand your grasp of emotional intelligence to boost your ability to navigate and master a broad variety of emotions?

_____

_____

_____

_____

_____

2. What thought patterns lead to the creation of particular emotions in different settings, and how can you grow awareness and control over these thoughts?

_____

_____

_____

_____

_____

_____

3. In what ways can you develop a stronger mind-body connection to allow greater emotional control and mastery?

_____

_____

_____

_____

_____

_____

_____

4. How can you reframe problems as chances for emotional development and resilience, enabling them to contribute positively to your overall well-being?

_____

_____

_____

_____

_____

_____

5. What healthy outlets can you add into your life for expressing and processing emotions, guaranteeing a more balanced and genuine emotional experience?

_____

_____

_____

_____

_____

_____

_____

_____

_____

_____

_____

_____

_____

FOOD FOR THOUGHT

1. Consider considering your emotions as useful instructors on your path. How can you draw lessons from both happy and negative emotions to drive your personal growth?

2. Reflect on how managing your emotions positively improves your relationships with others. How might your emotional intelligence aid to creating stronger connections and understanding?

3. Ponder on the delicate interplay between your mind and body in emotional events. How can you develop this relationship to achieve general well-being and emotional balance?

4. Explore the notion that emotional mastery leads to enhanced resilience. How might your capacity to handle emotions lead to a more robust and flexible mindset?

5. Consider the difficult balance between expressing and controlling emotions. How do you achieve a harmonic balance that allows for honest emotional expression while preserving productive communication?

KEYNOTES

Physically: Know Yourself

Key Lessons:

1. Recognize that your body works as a strong communicator, delivering insights into your general well-being. Cultivate awareness of bodily cues and symptoms to grasp your body's language.

2. Understand the value of holistic health in self-discovery. Embrace a complete approach that covers physical, mental, and emotional well-being for a more thorough knowledge of oneself.

3. Explore the complicated link between diet and cognitive performance. Recognize how the nutrients you eat directly impact your brain's function, altering your thoughts, emotions, and general clarity.

4. Delve into the relationship between physical exercise and mental resiliency. Appreciate the significance of exercise in nurturing not just physical health but also mental strength and emotional well-being.

5. Acknowledge the vital function of sleep in self-care. Understand how healthy sleep relates to cognitive performance, emotional management, and general physical and mental vigor.

Self-Refelction Questions:

1. How can you strengthen your capacity to read the information your body is giving, obtaining greater insights into your general well-being?

_____

_____

_____

_____

_____

2. In what ways can you incorporate a holistic approach to health, addressing not just physical but also mental and emotional components, to create a more thorough self-understanding?

_____

_____

_____

_____

_____

_____

3. How can you make more attentive decisions in your eating to maximize cognitive performance and promote your brain's health?

_____

_____

_____

_____

_____

4. How can you include physical exercise into your routine to not only boost physical health but also develop mental resilience and emotional well-being?

_____

_____

_____

_____

_____

5. What modifications can you make in your sleep pattern to emphasize excellent sleep, acknowledging its role in supporting your cognitive, emotional, and physical well-being?

_____

_____

_____

_____

_____

_____

_____

_____

_____

_____

_____

_____

_____

FOOD FOR THOUGHT

1. Reflect on the great knowledge contained in your body's intellect. How can you acknowledge and listen to these bodily signs as a roadmap to improved self-awareness?

2. Ponder on the delicate balance necessary for comprehensive well-being. How can you guarantee that your concentration on physical health seamlessly combines with mental and emotional well-being?

3. Consider the thought of nourishment as fuel for your brain. How can attentive dietary choices boost not just your physical health but also your cognitive and emotional well-being?

4. Explore the relationship between exercise and mental resiliency. How can physical exercise become a cornerstone in your routine for growing both physical and mental strength?

5. Reflect on sleep as a core part of self-care. How can prioritizing excellent sleep positively affect your capacity to know oneself on a deeper level?

KEYNOTES

_____

_____

_____

_____

_____

_____

_____

_____

_____

_____

_____

_____

_____

_____

Intuition: Trust Your Gut

Key Lessons:

1. Understand that intuition is your inner knowledge, a source of direction that transcends rationality. Embrace the concept that tapping into this inner wisdom may lead to more honest and aligned judgments.

2. Recognize that growing intuition needs heightened self-awareness. By being connected to your thoughts, emotions, and body sensations, you may increase your intuitive insights.

3. Explore the interesting gut-brain relationship. Understand how the stomach functions as a second brain, affecting your intuition and delivering crucial insights beyond conscious mental processes.

4. Appreciate the significance of blending intuition with logic. Strive for a harmonic blending of both ways of thinking, enabling intuition to complement and improve your decision-making.

5. Embrace the concept that intuition typically functions in its own time. Learn to trust the subtle cues and nudges, realizing that intuitive ideas may emerge gradually.

Self-Refelction Questions:

1. How can you develop your connection with your inner knowledge, creating a greater reliance on intuitive insights in your decision-making?

_____

_____

_____

_____

_____

_____

2. In what ways can you heighten your self-awareness to better tune into the subtle cues and signals that follow intuitive insights?

_____

_____

_____

_____

_____

_____

3. How can you actively listen to your gut instincts, appreciating the knowledge they carry, and incorporate this insight into your decision-making process?

_____

_____

_____

_____

_____

_____

4. How do you achieve a balance between intellectual analysis and intuitive impulses, enabling both to guide your judgments in a balanced manner?

_____

_____

_____

_____

_____

_____

5. How can you foster patience and confidence in the timing of intuitive insights, realizing that they may emerge gradually rather than in an instant?

_____

_____

_____

_____

_____

_____

_____

_____

_____

_____

_____

_____

FOOD FOR THOUGHT

1. Reflect on the wonder and enchantment inherent in intuition. How can you accept the unknown and allow intuition to lead you through the uncertainties of life?

2. Ponder on the thought that your intuition has great insight. How do you recognize and respect this wellspring of inner intellect in your everyday life?

3. Consider incorporating intuition into your daily decision-making. How may subtle, intuitive nudges lead to more aligned and honest choices?

4. Explore the relationship between a clean stomach and mental clarity. How can supporting gut health favorably affect your capacity to think clearly and make intuitive decisions?

5. Reflect on intuition as a voyage of self-discovery. How can following your instincts lead to a greater knowledge of yourself and your unique path in life?

KEYNOTES

Motivation: Stay Resilient To Achieve Your Goals

Key Lessons:

1. Recognize the significance of knowing your particular motivators. Identify what actually motivates you and link your objectives with these internal sources of motivation for sustainable resilience.

2. Explore the function of dopamine in motivation. Understand how generating a positive feedback loop by recognizing little accomplishments may increase motivation and resilience throughout your trip.

3. Embrace a growth attitude as a basis for resilience. View problems as chances for learning and progress, cultivating an attitude that pulls you ahead in the face of failures.

4. Acknowledge the importance of social support on your motivation. Cultivate a network of folks that inspire and support you, giving a source of strength during hard times.

5. Learn to reconcile short-term satisfaction with long-term objectives. Striking this balance enables ongoing motivation by rewarding immediate successes while keeping your focus on the wider picture.

Self-Refelction Questions:

1. How can you expand your awareness of your intrinsic motivators to guarantee your objectives line with what actually drives and satisfies you?

_____

_____

_____

_____

2. How can you add moments of joy into your path, knowing the importance of dopamine in maintaining motivation by appreciating minor wins?

_____

_____

_____

_____

_____

_____

_____

3. In what ways can you build a growth mindset when confronted with problems, perceiving them as chances for learning and personal development?

_____

_____

_____

_____

_____

4. How can you deliberately develop a supporting network that uplifts and stimulates you, building a sturdy foundation for your journey?

_____

_____

_____

_____

_____

_____

5. How do you create a balance between celebrating quick wins and retaining focus on your long-term objectives, guaranteeing continued motivation?

FOOD FOR THOUGHT

1. Reflect on the invigorating energy of inner motivation. How can tapping into your real passions inspire a sustained and resilient drive towards your goals?

2. Ponder on the concept that celebrating progress promotes motivation. How can you incorporate a celebratory attitude into your routine to drive you forward?

3. Consider setbacks as stepping stones to achievement. How might reframing obstacles as chances for development enhance your resilience and determination?

4. Reflect on the rippling impact of good social support. How can your supporting network not only encourage you but also contribute to a communal climate of resilience?

5. Explore the art of patience in motivating. How might embracing the journey, with its highs and lows, help to a resilient and persistent pursuit of your goals?

KEYNOTES

Logic: Make Good Decisions

Key Lessons:

1. Understand the necessity of balancing emotion and rationality in decision-making. Recognize that a harmonic combination of both components leads to well-informed and sensible decisions.

2. Explore the neurobiology underlying decision-making. Understand the brain's functions and how expanding your grasp of these systems may lead to more effective and informed judgments.

3. Acknowledge typical cognitive biases that may impact your judgments. Learn to detect and counteract these biases to make choices that correspond more closely with your aims and beliefs.

4. Embrace reflective thought as a strong tool in decision-making. Cultivate the practice of standing back to examine events objectively, allowing for more considered and smart decisions.

5. Recognize intuition as a rational tool. Understand that well-developed intuition is typically a product of collected information and experience, adding to the logic of your decision-making process.

Self-Refelction Questions:

1. How can you measure and regulate the role of emotions in your decision-making, guaranteeing a balanced and rational approach?

_____

_____

_____

_____

2. In what ways can you strengthen your knowledge of the brain processes involved in decision-making, allowing for more informed and purposeful choices?

_____

_____

_____

_____

_____

_____

3. How can you actively recognize and eliminate cognitive biases in your decision-making, creating a more objective and reasonable thinking process?

_____

_____

_____

_____

_____

_____

4. How can you build a habit of reflective thought, allowing for a more deliberate and strategic approach to your decisions?

_____

_____

_____

_____

_____

_____

5. How do you cultivate and trust your intuition, knowing it as a rational tool that draws from your gathered

_____

_____

_____

_____

_____

_____

_____

_____

_____

_____

_____

_____

_____

FOOD FOR THOUGHT

1. Reflect on the dynamic interplay between emotion and logic. How do you manage this dance to make choices that correspond with both your intellectual knowledge and emotional intelligence?

2. Ponder on the thought that knowing the neurobiology of decision-making empowers you. How may this understanding boost your capacity to make well-informed choices?

3. Consider biases as masks that impair decision clarity. How might uncovering and resolving these biases offer a new degree of transparency and objectivity to your choices?

4. Explore reflective thinking as a navigator in decision-making. How can this practice help you through challenging circumstances, providing a mindful and purposeful way forward?

5. Consider intuition as a silent logic. How might recognizing and trusting your intuition help to a more sophisticated and thorough decision-making process?

KEYNOTES

Creativity: Design Your Ideal Future

Key Lessons:

1. Recognize the potential of creative expression as a tool for constructing your ideal future. Understand how participating in creative activities may uncover inventive thoughts and determine your way ahead.

2. Explore the notion of neuroplasticity as a catalyst for releasing your creative potential. Understand how the brain's malleability allows for the continuing growth of creative talents and ideas.

3. Acknowledge the importance of positive vision on your creative process. Learn how imagining your ideal future may inspire and direct your creative attempts toward creating that vision.

4. Understand the significance of creative cooperation in building your future. Explore how varied viewpoints and collaborative efforts may strengthen your creative thinking and contribute to your ambitions.

5. Embrace the significance of building a creative attitude. Recognize that an inquisitive and open response to difficulties encourages creativity, helping you to construct a future full with possibilities.

Self-Refelction Questions:

1. How can you select and participate in creative activities that connect with you, enabling you to express yourself and form your vision for the future?

_____

_____

_____

_____

_____

2. In what ways can you actively tap into the neuroplasticity of your brain, enabling continual growth and development of your creative skills?

_____

_____

_____

_____

_____

_____

3. How can you apply positive visualization into your routine to visualize and construct your perfect future, matching your creative efforts with your aspirations?

_____

_____

_____

_____

_____

4. How can you seek and welcome creative partnerships that provide new views and ideas, improving your creative process and contributing to your future plans?

_____

_____

_____

_____

_____

5. What behaviors can you embrace to promote a creative mindset, cultivating curiosity, openness, and flexibility as you create your path toward an ideal future?

_____

_____

_____

_____

_____

_____

_____

_____

_____

_____

_____

_____

_____

FOOD FOR THOUGHT

1. Reflect on creativity as a lifetime friend. How can you combine creative thinking into every part of your life, continually shaping your path toward an ideal future?

2. Ponder on the thought that your brain's neuroplasticity is a creative playground. How can you explore and exploit this playground to continually enhance and expand your creative abilities?

3. Consider the magnetic force of optimistic vision in creative undertakings. How might your envisioned perfect future work as a magnetic force, directing and drawing you toward its realization?

4. Explore cooperation as a fuel for invention. How might the synergy of varied minds contribute to the imaginative design of your future, bringing out unique and transforming ideas?

5. Contemplate creativity as a mentality rather than a talent. How can adopting a creative mentality become a basic part in your approach to difficulties, progress, and the pursuit of your ideal future?

KEYNOTES

Step 1: Raised Awareness – Switch Off Your Autopilot

Key Lessons:

1. Embrace the concept that mindful living unleashes your entire potential. By shutting off autopilot, you enable yourself to participate with life more purposefully, enabling development and satisfaction.

2. Recognize mindfulness as the cure to autopilot life. Integrate mindfulness activities into your everyday routine to create present-moment awareness and break free from habitual reactions.

3. Understand the significance of unconscious tendencies on your life. Raised awareness helps you to detect and alter these tendencies, leading to more purposeful and good consequences.

4. Explore how using your senses promotes consciousness. Embrace the diversity of sensory stimuli to anchor yourself in the present moment and heighten your overall awareness.

5. Acknowledge that enhanced awareness helps you to regain control. By getting off autopilot, you become an active participant in molding your experiences, choices, and eventually, your life.

Self-Refelction Questions:

1. How do you recognize and become aware of the autopilot behaviors that may be restricting your potential and hampering conscious living?

_____

_____

_____

_____

_____

2. In what ways can you inject mindfulness into your ordinary moments to build a heightened awareness of your thoughts, feelings, and actions?

_____

_____

_____

_____

_____

_____

3. How can you discover and bring awareness to unconscious patterns that may be impacting your choices and actions without your conscious knowledge?

_____

_____

_____

_____

_____

_____

4. How can you intentionally engage your senses as a doorway to heightened awareness, enabling you to enjoy and appreciate each moment more fully?

_____

_____

_____

_____

_____

_____

5. How does spreading awareness enable you to take charge of your life? In what ways may deliberate living contribute to a more meaningful and purposeful existence?

_____

_____

_____

_____

_____

_____

_____

_____

_____

_____

_____

_____

FOOD FOR THOUGHT

1. Contemplate the thought that there is a better and more rewarding existence beyond autopilot. How may adopting higher awareness bring you towards a more purposeful and meaningful existence?

2. Reflect on mindfulness as a storehouse of current moments. How might tapping into this reservoir improve your everyday experiences and contribute to a more aware and deliberate life?

3. Ponder on the tapestry of unconscious patterns in your life. How might unraveling and changing these tendencies lead to a more purposeful and positive life story?

4. Explore the notion of sensory awareness as a pathway to the present moment. How does completely immersing oneself in the variety of sensory experiences boost your overall awareness?

5. Consider mindful life as a source of empowerment. How can increased awareness and getting off autopilot enable you to design your life in accordance with your beliefs and aspirations?

KEYNOTES

Step 2: Action Board It

Key Lessons:

1. Understand that action boards bring clarity to your vision. By turning your consciousness into real pictures and objectives, you build a compelling visual depiction of your desires.

2. Recognize visualization as a way to activate your brain. Action boards excite your brain, reaffirming your objectives and teaching your mind to work towards making your dreams into reality.

3. Embrace the concept that action boards empower your everyday decisions. By keeping your objectives visually visible, you may match your everyday activities with your long-term goals, creating consistency and growth.

4. Explore the science underlying goal reinforcement. Action boards utilize the brain's neurological connections to reinforce your objectives, generating a strong synergy between your ideas, actions, and successes.

5. Acknowledge that action boards help you break down ambitions into practical actions. By concentrating on concrete tasks, you may convert abstract concepts into doable milestones, encouraging the development of your vision.

Self-Refelction Questions:

1. How can you utilize action boards to clarify and graphically portray your vision, generating a concrete map that leads your path towards your goals?

_____

_____

_____

_____

_____

2. In what ways can you engage your brain more effectively via visualization on action boards, reinforcing your objectives and training your mind for success?

_____

_____

_____

_____

_____

3. How can you guarantee that your everyday decisions correspond with the visual representations on your action boards, establishing a consistent and purposeful route towards your aspirations?

---

4. How does knowing the neurological science underpinning goal reinforcement change your approach to constructing action boards and visualizing your goals?

---

5. How can you utilize action boards to break down your objectives into clear, practical stages, reducing abstract ideals into actionable and attainable milestones?

_____

_____

_____

_____

_____

_____

_____

_____

_____

_____

_____

_____

FOOD FOR THOUGHT

1. Reflect on action boards as imaginative blueprints. How might this concrete depiction of your objectives serve as a daily reminder and guidance for your road toward success?

2. Ponder on the harmony between imagery and the strength of your brain. How can the combination of action boards and neural reinforcement move you towards the achievement of your aspirations?

3. Consider everyday decisions as the building blocks of your success. How can aligning your choices with the images on your action board contribute to the steady construction of your desired future?

4. Explore the dance of neural pathways in goal achievement. How can understanding and leveraging neural science through action boards enhance the efficiency and effectiveness of your path to success?

5. Contemplate tangible steps as the bridge between your vision and reality. How can breaking down your aspirations into actionable steps on action boards pave the way for the manifestation of your dreams?

KEYNOTES

Step 3: Focused Attention – Neuroplasticity In Action

Key Lessons:

1. Understand that concentrated attention actively alters your brain circuits. By focusing your attention consciously, you sculpt the structure of your brain, impacting your ideas, habits, and general mentality.

2. Embrace the notion of neuroplasticity as the flexibility of your brain. Recognize that with concentrated attention, you may rewire your brain, promoting good changes and personal development.

3. Explore mindfulness as a great tool for neuroplasticity. Cultivating a conscious presence in your everyday life helps you to change your brain's structure in accordance with your objectives and desires.

4. Acknowledge that where you concentrate your attention forms your reality. Focused attention effects not just your internal cognitive processes but also how you see and interact with the external environment.

5. Understand that sustained concentrated attention produces competence. Whether learning a new skill or cultivating good habits, persistent attention and practice lead to mastery and competence.

Self-Refelction Questions:

1. How can you use your concentrated attention to actively modify your brain pathways, supporting beneficial changes in your ideas, habits, and mindset?

_____

_____

_____

_____

2. In what ways can you incorporate mindfulness into your everyday life, leveraging its neuroplasticity-enhancing abilities to align your brain with your intended goals?

_____

_____

_____

_____

_____

3. How does the knowledge of where you put your attention effect your internal cognitive processes and your exterior interactions with the world around you?

_____

_____

_____

_____

_____

4. How might constant and focused attention help to gaining knowledge and mastery in areas important to you, encouraging development and proficiency?

_____

_____

_____

_____

_____

5. How does knowing the flexibility of your brain via neuroplasticity encourage you to actively modify your brain's structure in accordance with your aspirations?

_____

_____

_____

_____

_____

_____

_____

_____

_____

_____

_____

_____

_____

FOOD FOR THOUGHT

1. Reflect on concentrated attention as the sculptor of your cerebral environment. How can you actively change your brain's structure to create a mental environment that matches with your intended future?

2. Ponder on mindfulness as a strong elixir for good development. How might the purposeful practice of mindfulness boost your potential to remodel your brain connections and generate personal growth?

3. Consider attention as the painter of your world. How can actively directing your concentration impact not just your internal world but also your perception and experience of the exterior world?

4. Explore the connection between continuous attention and skill. How can continuous attention and practice blend to produce a masterpiece of mastery in areas important to you?

5. Contemplate neuroplasticity as the open arms of transformation. How might knowing your brain's flexibility allow you to actively engage in the constant growth of your ideas and abilities?

KEYNOTES

Step 4: Deliberate Practice – The Source Comes To Life

Key Lessons:

1. Understand that deliberate practice is the key to refining your talents. By participating in focused, purposeful, and systematic practice, you increase your talents and grow closer to embodying your preferred self.

2. Embrace the function of feedback in your focused practice. Constructive criticism functions as a guiding force, delivering insights that move you ahead on your road toward fulfilling your objectives.

3. Explore how conscious repetition helps to mastery. Deliberate practice is deliberate repetition with complete awareness, helping you to perfect your talents and increase your knowledge.

4. Acknowledge that focused practice includes welcoming problems. Through overcoming problems and stretching your limitations, you spark personal and professional progress, bringing your dreams to reality.

5. Recognize that consistency is the cornerstone of focused practice. Regular, concentrated work over time is the key for changing your potential into realized talents and bringing "The Source" inside you to life.

Self-Refelction Questions:

1. How can you apply the concepts of deliberate practice to your objectives, ensuring that your efforts are intentional, focused, and contribute to your skill development?

_____

_____

_____

_____

2. How can you establish an atmosphere that accepts constructive criticism, recognizing it as a vital guide in your path of focused practice and personal growth?

_____

_____

_____

_____

_____

_____

3. In what ways can you inject mindfulness into your repetitions during purposeful practice, ensuring that each repetition leads to a greater knowledge and mastery of your skills?

_____

_____

_____

_____

_____

4. How can you actively welcome setbacks as chances for progress within your intentional practice, acknowledging that overcoming difficulties is vital to fulfilling your aspirations?

_____

_____

_____

_____

_____

5. How can you create consistency in your purposeful practice, making it a habit that maintains your growth and adds to the constant unfolding of your potential?

FOOD FOR THOUGHT

1. Reflect on purposeful practice as the canvas where your talents and abilities are methodically painted. How can you utilize this canvas to construct a masterpiece that resonates with your aspirations?

2. Ponder on feedback as the sculptor's chisel. How can you accept feedback as an instrument that develops and refines your talents, bringing you closer to the accomplishment of your goals?

3. Consider repetition as the rhythmic pulse of expertise. How might the conscious repetition inherent in purposeful practice lead to a symphony of skill growth and greater understanding?

4. Explore difficulties as catalysts for change. How might meeting and conquering problems in your intentional practice be understood as stepping stones toward the lively expression of your aspirations?

5. Contemplate consistency as the sustaining factor in your focused practice. How may adopting a consistent and deliberate approach lead to the constant blossoming of your potential and the vivid realization of "The Source" inside you?

KEYNOTES

KEYNOTES

KEYNOTES

KEYNOTES

Made in the USA
Las Vegas, NV
20 October 2024

10131352R00074